Pond creatures usually need to stay by water.

Animals like rabbits will burrow anywhere they can.

Have a look in a pond, around a field and in the woods to find out where creatures live. Make a chart to show what you find out.

Here is the chart I made.

Glossary: **Habitat** – the natural home of an animal or plant.

3

What do animals need?

Look at some pictures of animals that live nearby and choose which ones you will find out about.

Find where the animals live.

Outdoor Explorers
Shelters and Habitats

By Sandy Green   Photography by Chris Fairclough

Contents

W
FRANKLIN WATTS

What are habitats?

Every living thing has a habitat that is best for them. This includes their home and the sort of place they like to be.

Most birds nest in trees and prefer wooded areas.

What do you think they need?

For example:
- a rabbit needs a burrow and plants to eat.

- a worm needs damp soil.

What other things
might they need?

Make a nest

Think about nests and talk about how they keep birds, mice and other small creatures both safe and warm.

Collect twigs and sticks and form them into nest shapes by weaving them through each other.

Next, look for soft things to line the nests. Feathers, wool, moss and leaves can work well.

We think our nest is cosy and warm.

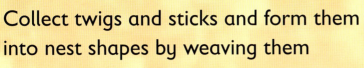

Glossary: **Weaving** – linking things together by going in and out or under and over.

Make a birdfeeder

Birds like to eat insects, nuts and seeds.

- Use halves of coconut shells to make a birdfeeder.

- Get an adult to make a hole near the edge of each shell.

- Tie string through each hole.

- Mix peanuts, pumpkin or sunflower seeds, bird seed and cooking fat together, and then press the mixture into each coconut shell.

- Hang the shells in trees or from a fence.

Watch the birds as they come to feed. Why do you think it is especially important to feed birds in the winter?

Make an animal shelter

With some friends, make shelters for small animals to hibernate in. Collect twigs, stones, leaves, feathers, mud and moss.

- Build a pile of each material you have collected.

- Place a cup of warm water into each of them.

- Measure the temperature of the water with a thermometer.

Later on, measure the temperatures again to see which shelter stayed the warmest. Was it the one you thought it would be?

Why do you think some animals hibernate?

Glossary: **Hibernate** – to sleep through the winter.

What's in the pond?

The best ponds have a shallow area to help frogs, toads and newts to climb in and out.

They have a deep area for fish to swim and hide in too.

Watch carefully to see
what is coming and going.

Reeds are a good place to
spot dragonflies and damselflies.

Draw a picture of a pond.

What's your favourite
pond creature? Why?

Do you like our
pond pictures?

Wattle and daub shelter

Build a small shelter using sticks, mud, water and straw. This is called wattle and daub.

People need homes, too. What do our homes need to be like?

- Push a circle of wooden stakes into the ground. Weave sticks around the circle to create wattle.

- Make another circle in the same way outside the first circle. Stuff straw in between the circles for warmth.

• Mix mud, straw and water to form daub and fill in the gaps.

• Make a roof using leafy branches.

People used to make homes in this way. What would it be like to live in a wattle and daub home?

Glossary: **Stake** – a wooden stick with a pointed end.

A dry shelter

We need to stay dry in wet weather.

Make a shelter to keep you dry by using rope and tarpaulin. Tarpaulin is a heavy material that does not let the rain in.

- Find an area of trees or strong branches where you can tie the tarpaulin across.

- Work with friends to spread the tarpaulin out flat, fixing it as high as you can make it.

- Fix it securely at all four corners.
- Find something soft to sit on inside your shelter.

I collected leaves to sit on.

You can also make a tent using three large branches tied at the top with the tarpaulin over them.

How could you make your shelter better?

Build a teepee

Some Native Americans used to live in shelters called teepees.

- Collect three or four sticks to make a teepee.

- The sticks need to be as tall as you are and nearly as thick as your arms.

- Tie the sticks together at the top with rope and spread the sticks out in a circle at the bottom. This shape is now like a teepee.

- Cover your teepee with an old blanket or sheet.

- Sit inside your teepee and listen to stories about Native Americans.

Would you like to live in a teepee? Why?

Get cooking!

Get an adult to light a small fire outdoors.

- Make your own cooking tool. Find a fallen stick from a hazel tree, about twice as long as your arm, and take off the leaves.

- Use a potato peeler to peel the bark off one end of the stick.

- Twist a 'snake' of dough or a marshmallow onto the end of your stick.

Always listen carefully and work safely. No pushing or running.

• Hold it over the fire like a fork.

• Wrap small potatoes in foil and ask an adult to put them in the fire to cook.

These taste yummy!

Activity ideas

What are habitats? (pages 2-3)
- How many different habitats can children think of?
- What are the main differences in the needs of people, birds, animals and plants?
- Introduce words such as burrow, sett and drey.

What do animals need? (pages 4-5)
- Make a list of woodland animals with the children. Allocate each child an animal to find out about.
- Help each child explore what their animal's needs are: food, shelter, bedding, safety etc.
- Provide pictures of animals.

Make a nest (pages 6-7)
- Talk about nests and who makes them.
- Talk about when nests are built and where, e.g. birds mostly nest in trees and hedgerows, mice and rabbits nest underground.
- Explore the textures of natural items such as feathers, moss and leaves. Which feel softest? Introduce as many descriptive words as you can.
- Which textures would the children choose to sleep on?

Make a birdfeeder (pages 8-9)
- Talk about the importance of continuity; how birds come to the garden expecting to find food and what might happen if they don't find any.
- Talk about the need for different types of birdfeeders for different types of birds - how some birds are ground feeders and some feed from hanging feeders.
- Encourage the children to put out juicy fruits such as grapes and apples and observe which birds eat them.
- Encourage children to observe where else birds find food e.g. worms and insects, berries on plants etc.
- Talk about the colour, size and shapes of the birds.

Make an animal shelter (pages 10-11)
- Talk about how important it is for animals (people included) to live in suitable temperatures.
- Do the children prefer to be cold, warm or hot? Why?
- Explore the children's thinking about which type of nest will be the warmest.
- Use the downloadable temperature chart to keep measurements of how warm each nest was.

What's in the pond? (pages 12-13)
- Talk about safety around deep water.
- Talk about the differences between frogs, newts and toads; how they move, where they go, what they eat.
- Explore why fish need deeper water. What might happen if it was too shallow in winter or in summer?

- Ask the children to draw or paint a dragonfly and create waterlily pictures with collage materials.
- Show them a copy of a Monet waterlily painting and talk about it with them. Can they paint like Monet?
- Talk about how charcoal is made and how this is a natural material. Use charcoal to create pictures of the pond. How does is differ from using a pencil?

Wattle and daub shelter (pages 14-15)
- Talk about the different types of homes people live in. What are they like? What things are essential?
- How do the needs of people differ from animals?
- Explore with the children what it would be like to live outdoors. Who has been camping? What did they like/dislike about it? Would they like to live like that all the time? Why?
- Ask the children to design a shelter that they would like to live in. Discuss their chosen features. Which would be essential to them?
- Hazel sticks work well for the shelter because they grow long and straight and grow fast so regenerate quickly.

A dry shelter (pages 16-17)
- Talk about why we need to stay dry. Who has got very wet when outdoors? How did it make them feel?
- Who can tie a knot? How tight can they make it? Would it be tight enough to make a shelter secure? Why would this be important?

Build a teepee (pages 18-19)
- Talk about Native Americans. Who has heard stories or seen films about them? What can they tell you about how they live?
- Has anyone ever been in a teepee? What was it like?
- Read stories about Native Americans to the children.
- Talk about totem poles and how Native Americans used to carve these and dance around them.
- Make a totem pole for outside their teepee, using boxes and other 'junk', tied to a pole or post.
- Help the children create a totem pole dance.

Get cooking! (pages 20-21)
- Explain how to light a fire safely. How might the weather affect this?
- Talk about safety when near to fires.
- Draw up a list of fire safety rules with the children.
- Make a simple bread mix ready for cooking.
- How might the weather affect how well the fire cooks the food?
- Sing camp fire songs after eating the cooked food.

About this book

Each book in this series provides opportunities to enhance learning and development, supporting the four main principles of the early years foundation stage: a unique child, positive relationships, enabling environments, learning and development.

Children who are given opportunities to try, to explore, to find out about their environment and to learn through both success and error will become resilient, capable, confident and self-assured. The outdoor environment is very much an enabling environment. It provides different approaches to learning in which most children thrive, with many developing greater levels of concentration and engagement in activities than they may demonstrate indoors. The freedom of the outdoors encourages positive relationships in children with both their peers and with adults, and develops independence and inner strength. All six areas of learning and development are supported across the activities in this series. Examples of these can be seen in the charts provided at www.franklinwatts.co.uk.

The activities in this book automatically lend themselves to the introduction of new language, thinking points and questioning. They encourage exploration and investigation, both as an individual, and jointly with others. Many activities can be adapted further to meet specific learning needs.

Further information

Free downloadable activity sheets
Go to www.franklinwatts.co.uk to find these free downloadable activity sheets that accompany the activities:

• A temperature chart to keep measurements of how warm each nest is (pages 10-11).

• An identification chart for pond minibeasts (pages 12-13).

Forest Schools
The philosophy of Forest Schools is to encourage and inspire individuals of any age through positive outdoor experiences. Go to the website to find out about what happens at a Forest School, find one local to you, learn how to set one up and more.

www.forestschools.com

Index

This edition published in 2013
by Franklin Watts

Copyright © Franklin Watts 2013

Franklin Watts
338 Euston Road
London NW1 3BH

Franklin Watts Australia
Level 17/207 Kent Street
Sydney, NSW 2000

All rights reserved.

Series editor: Sarah Peutrill
Art director: Jonathan Hair
Designer: Jane Hawkins
Photography: Chris Fairclough,
unless otherwise stated

Dewey number: 643.1
ISBN: 978 1 4451 1961 8

Credits: Jonathan Clark/istockphoto: 6b.
S Eyerkaufer/Shutterstock: 12b. Andrew
Howe/istockphoto: 9t, 13t. Igorsky/
Shutterstock: 2c. K Kymek/Shutterstock:
13c. One Small Square/Shutterstock:
18t. Lincoln Rogers/Shutterstock 5cl.
RT Images/Shutterstock: 6c. Sally Scott/
Shutterstock: 16t. Vitaly Titov &
Maris Sidelnikova/Shutterstock: 2b.
Irina Tschenko/Shutterstock: 12t.
Vinicius Tupinamba/Shutterstock: 4t,
5cr. Vasily Vishnevskiy/Shutterstock: 2t.
Xtremer/Shutterstock: 6t. Every attempt
has been made to clear copyright.
Should there be any inadvertent
omission please apply to the publisher
for rectification.

Franklin Watts is a division of Hachette
Children's Books, an Hachette UK
company. www.hachette.co.uk

The Author and Publisher would like
to thank Karen Constable, reception
class teacher at Mark First School in
Somerset, for her suggestions and help
with this series. Also thanks to the
school, especially the children, for their
enthusiasm, cooperation and sense of
fun during the photoshoots.

Printed in China

Important note: an adult should
supervise the activities in this
book, especially those near water
and fire.